DROPSHIPPING

6 STEPS TO START A SUCCESSFUL DROPSHIP ECOMMERCE BUSINESS AND OPTIMIZATION STRATEGIES TO 10X YOUR STORE PROFITS

Copyright © Richard Wall 2017
All Rights Reserved.

Table of Contents

Introduction 7
What Are The Advantages Of Dropshipping? 10
Different Methods of Dropshipping 14
Choosing a Niche and Products to Sell 29
Finding and Contacting Suppliers 35
Creating a Dropshipping Website 43
Store Checklist 54
How to Fulfill Orders 65
How to Automate Your Store 80
Marketing Your Store 92
Other Ways to Boost Sales 116
Exit Strategy 123
Conclusion 131

Introduction

Dropshipping is an online retailing business model where the seller sells products on the internet but they do not hold or invest in the stock upfront. In simple terms, this means that the seller does not handle the fulfillment. For instance, when an ecommerce store sells an item, the store owner then purchases the item from a third party seller and has it directly shipped to their customer. A person who runs a dropshipping business is known as a dropshipper.

A lot of people get confused when it comes to understanding the basics of dropshipping. It is much easier to explain when it is compared with conventional retailing. The main difference between dropshipping and standard retailing is that in dropshipping, the seller does not stock the inventory. A small-scale ecommerce business loves dropshipping because there is only a small upfront investment required due to the fact that there is no need for inventory.

Dropshipping is a relatively new fulfillment method, however, over the recent years we have seen an increase in the amount websites and suppliers who now dropship. Globalization has played a critical role in the growth of dropshipping activities, allowing for dropshippers to source Chinese manufactured products a lot easier.

Dropshipping requires the seller to focus most of his/her efforts in marketing the store. The marketing part is probably the most pivotal aspect of dropshipping. If you do not properly market your business you have slim chances of achieving success in this field. There are dozens of techniques that you can apply in a dropshipping business and most of them involve using popular social media platforms and search engines such as Google.

What Are The Advantages Of Dropshipping?

There are a lot of advantages with being a dropshipper. The biggest advantage dropshipping has over regular ecommerce retailing is that dropshippers do not have the high start-up costs of a regular seller who would need to rent a store or location and then purchase the products from suppliers. Dropshippers do not need a physical store as all of their selling will be done online. This saves the dropshipper a lot of money when starting a dropshipping business meaning anyone with a tight budget can start a successful store in a small amount of time.

Dropshippers also have access to millions of products, unlike standard retailers who first need to purchase their products, before they can sell. This can allow dropshippers to react to trends more quickly and provide a better offering to potential customers.

To put it in perspective, imagine a retailer who sells coffee machines online and in a physical store. This retailer will be limited due to space; therefore, he/she can only afford to sell a certain number or types of coffee machines. However, a dropshipper can simply find the suppliers of all the products which he wants to sell online and offer them to his/her customer. The dropshipper is not limited by space. Having a broad selection of products can certainly give you an edge over a more conventional store.

In terms of time management, dropshipping tends to be a lot more time effective for the seller. Whilst it tends to take the same amount of time to post products that you have in inventory as it will take to post products that you intend to dropship.

Dropshipping removes the need for shipping products from the producer or supplier to the seller. This makes it easier to dropship goods and it also saves time as there is no need to ship goods to the online retailer. Dropshipping also tends to be less time consuming due to the fact that the merchant does not need to receive stock or package and ship products to customers. These tasks are time-consuming and costly. Imagine having to package a hundred orders and ship them to customers. With dropshipping, the dropshipper doesn't have to worry about the fulfillment as they are handled by the supplier and shipped directly to the customer.

It will probably take you a few weeks to start an online store that sells physically stocked products. Due to the fact that dropshipping is semi-automated, this makes it a lot more hassle-free and less time consuming to start. A seller can get started with dropshipping very quickly and his/her site can be reached by thousands of prospective buyers within a few hours.

Dropshipping is also location independent as most of the business transactions are done online. The dropshipper can send products to any part of the globe without having to hold the product. Dropshipping location independent model makes it a very lucrative business model to venture into, as you can run your business from anywhere in the world as long as you have internet access.

Different Methods of Dropshipping

Now let us focus on the different methods of dropshipping. The principals of dropshipping are usually the same but dropshipping can be done in a number of different ways. Depending on your experience you might choose a certain form of dropshipping. All of these different types of dropshipping methods fall into two types of categories, namely straight or blind dropshipping.

Straight Dropshipping

Straight dropshipping involves the supplier having to promote their websites. This kind of dropshipping is important when you have to sell a product that you do not want to offer any customer support for. This means that any warrant will have to be taken directly with the supplier and not the dropshipper. In this case, the supplier will have his/her branding on the packaging of the product. This kind of dropshipping is more hassle-free as the supplier tends to be more involved in the whole process.

Blind Dropshipping

This is the more common of the two types of dropshipping. In this kind of dropshipping, the dropshipper does not provide their details, but directly ships products to the customer's address. This form of dropshipping is called blind dropshipping because both the customer and the supplier have no direct connection. Usually, when the product is shipped, the customer will think it's the dropshipper who shipped it from their warehouse. The dropshipper, in this case, deals directly with the customer's question, queries, and returns.

After looking at the main types of dropshipping it will be a disservice to the reader not to focus on other forms of dropshipping. When I say other forms of dropshipping I am talking about the main methods. Here will be looking at the broad types of dropshipping and their advantages. This includes popular dropshipping methods that involve Amazon, eBay, and Aliexpress.

Amazon To eBay Arbitrage

Amazon has become one of the most popular online ecommerce destinations around the world for buyers and sellers. This has caused the online marketplace to become a global corporate giant. Amazon currently has a value of almost half a trillion dollars and some speculators have stated that it is likely to reach a value of one trillion over the next decade. eBay, which is a very popular seller to seller marketplace, also has millions of users every month. This has strategically made these markets targets for dropshipping activities. Arbitrage in simple terms is taking advantage of differences in market prices. Due to the fact that prices on eBay and Amazon are usually different, dropshippers have taken advantage of this difference and taken to selling (dropshipping) Amazon products on eBay. This has become a lucrative business for dropshippers and sellers. However, some sellers on Amazon have reported that arbitrage has become a liability for them.

A guy called "Steve" was working an 8-hour job every day. One day he decided to develop a product called the scrub–scrub. This product was excellent in cleaning surfaces such as tiles and granite. He then decided to sell the product after quitting his job. The most popular marketplace was Amazon so he decided that he was going to begin selling his product on Amazon. After hiring a factory to manufacture the product he posted the product on Amazon. Sales started to increase every month. He was making a profit after a few months.

One day his friend came to tell him that he had seen this product being sold on eBay. Steve reluctantly went on eBay and he discovered that it was true and there were many sellers selling his product on eBay at different prices. Immediately, he thought that someone in the factory was stealing his product and selling it online. The following day he went to the factory and confronted the manager, only to make a fool out of himself. He went home distressed and decided to purchase the product on eBay so that he can take a good look at it. He purchased the product on eBay only to receive an Amazon packaging. After doing a research on the issue, he discovered that the product was his own and the seller was actually dropshipping the product from Amazon, in return for a profit.

This was parasitical as the seller was making a living out of his hard work. After a few months, he started making losses due to arbitrage as customers were returning this product. He made losses of around $8000 in three months as customers made more than 90 returns from dropshippers. He tried contacting Amazon and eBay but got nowhere. He then tried to communicate with the dropshippers. This did not work either so he resorted to a new plan. He would also start selling his product on both Amazon and eBay in order to prevent sellers from dropshipping his product. As he was the owner of the product, he was able to list the product at the lowest price on eBay. Finally, he was making a profit again.

On Amazon or eBay, there is probably very little a seller can do to have a market advantage other than selling products at a lower cost. This kind of competition is the one that has driven most sellers to choose dropshipping. Dropshippers have the advantage of selling their products at a slightly higher price on eBay than Amazon. This price difference is the main factor behind arbitrage.

Marketing opportunities on large ecommerce marketplaces are very slim, therefore when dropshipping to eBay, you need to have one of the lowest prices on the marketplace. This makes your product more attractive to customers who would be willing to spend money on a bargain. Arbitrage in layman's terms can be referred to as harnessing the power of multibillion-dollar companies.

It should have already popped up in your mind that a customer purchasing a product on eBay and receiving an Amazon package could become aggravated. This is where you should provide an explanation to your customers. Smart customers will simply solve the equation themselves and go and search the product on Amazon. However, let's assume that they don't do this. You can simply explain to them that you use the Amazon fulfillment services. Some sellers simply tell their customers the truth and simplify things. This is not a good idea as the customer will most likely decide to go and purchase the product on Amazon next time or leave you a bad review. Luckily, the customer does not care in most cases and is just happy to receive the product that they ordered.

Aliexpress Dropshipping

Dropshippers have a large supply market to choose from so the market for new dropshippers might be a bit confusing or mysterious, so let's shed some light on the subject. Some dropshippers use Chinese suppliers. Chinese suppliers have become synonymous with dropshipping as a lot of dropshipped products are made in China. I know there is a negative stereotype about Chinese products as some people say they are low-quality products. This is of cause true about some Chinese products, but you should take note that even some products which are made in America are actually low-quality products as well. Therefore, China also has high-quality products. This means a dropshipper should know his/her products very well and assess the quality of all of their supplier's products. This eases the problem with dropshipping poor quality products.

The most popular supply marketplace currently for this type of method is Aliexpress. Aliexpress is a subsidiary of the company Alibaba, which was founded by Jack Ma after failing to find Chinese good on the internet. Aliexpress is the single largest inventory marketplace for dropshippers. On Aliexpress, dropshippers have the privilege to dropship millions of products located in a single market. Aliexpress has become synonymous with dropshipping. This is because of the availability of cheap products that the dropshipper can sell at a bargain price.

Some suppliers even know that their customers are actually dropshipping. This comes at a relief for dropshippers as the supplier usually does not put any label on the product to reveal where it is actually coming from. Unlike Amazon to eBay dropshipping where the customer receives a package which is labeled Amazon but he/she purchased the product on eBay.

I know what a lot of readers might be thinking on this topic. How long should the customer wait to receive the product if the product is being shipped from a Chinese supplier? The majority of the sales will be from customers in the USA. Luckily, China has a good relationship with the United States Postal Service and packages can be delivered from the factories in China direct to your customer in approximately 20-40 days. It can take up to 2 months to reach some customers overseas, depending on their location, however. I know a lot of dropshippers are questioning if the customer will be willing to wait that long for their product to be delivered. Most customers will actually be willing to wait for weeks as long as they think they are getting a bargain on their product.

This takes us to the next point about pricing your Aliexpress dropshipped goods. This is one of the most important factors in the dropshipping industry. The main advice here is you want to find products that are within a $1-$20 price range and are lightweight to ship. A good example would be to buy jewelry for $2 and sell for $20. This means you can afford to markup your price high in order to make a profit. You could, of course, sell the piece of jewelry for $4 and make $2 profit but it would take a lot more orders to make a significant amount of money and fulfilling orders is time-consuming for dropshippers. You also need to price the item low enough so that the customer thinks they are getting a bargain.

These days it has become simple for dropshippers to dropship through Aliexpress. However, it should be noted that this form of dropshipping involves tasks such as copying product descriptions and obtaining photographs of the product from the supplier. This makes it quite easy for dropshippers as they will only need to copy and paste most of the information to their websites. However, applications such as Oberlo have made it even easier for dropshippers. Dropshippers can now use Oberlo to import products from Aliexpress to their own websites. This comes as an advantage as it makes the whole process less labor intensive.

Manufacturer to Customer

Fortunately, you do not need to look as far as China to be able to successfully dropship online. Having a local supplier or manufacturer in your own country agree to deliver directly to your customer can be the most lucrative dropshipping method, as long as you choose the right products.

The manufacturer usually does not have time to market their product. This has made the dropshipper an irreplaceable part of the supply chain. For example, it is far cheaper and easier for a manufacturer to focus on producing the product than spending much of their time trying to market it. The dropshipper can focus on the marketing elements of the product better than the manufacturer and the dropshipper is merely taking a percentage for doing the marketing for them.

Another downside of direct selling by the manufacturer is that they have small coverage when selling the product. Limited coverage, especially for small manufacturers, makes it more convenient for them to use dropshippers and other retailers. On the side of the dropshipper, it is more advantageous for a dropshipper to ship products directly from the manufacturer to the customer because the product will most likely have a lower price, than using wholesalers. This means the dropshipper can offer the customer a bargain price.

Being an effective dropshipper involves having to choose the best manufacturers on the market. Also, you will need to be able to select the best products from these manufacturers so that your customers are pleased. It's important to note that establishing reliability and product quality is important for you and your customers as most customers are in fact return customers.

Establishing trust between the dropshipper and the manufacturer is also important as you can request certain things or terms from the manufacturer that ordinary buyers cannot.

Choosing a Niche and Products to Sell

This is the part that you should pay close attention to. The products that you sell when you start dropshipping are the ones that will guarantee your success or failure in the dropshipping market. Dropshipping requires you to have a keen eye as far as choosing products to add on your dropshipping store is concerned. Always make sure that the niche that you choose has to have fewer competitors on the market. There are some niche markets that are already flooded therefore selecting them will make it a lot more difficult for you to get any sales.

Choosing a niche is probably the first step in the ecommerce sector. Niche selection can either make or break a business. Therefore, you have to choose your niche more carefully if you are going to run a successful dropshipping business.

A Niche is a small specialized product trend or service. In this case, because we are focusing on dropshipping, a niche will be a specialized product trend. The reader should keep in mind that popular advertising platforms such as Facebook and Google ads increase the price of a product based on the niche that it belongs in. For example ads in the finance sector tend to be a lot more expensive. Therefore, when selecting a niche to focus on, the dropshipper should consider the total costs to market the product. This means that a thorough niche research will aid the dropshipper in finding out how competitive their niche is. The best advice is to focus on less competitive niches.

Google AdWords comes as one of the most effective online niche research tools. You can simply find out the ad cost of each keyword associated with your niche. Go to AdWords and search the competitiveness of your niche keyword. Many variants of your keyword will appear and AdWords will show you how competitive they are. This should not come as a surprise as this form of niche research is popular.

Some people may ask "Why don't I just sell all products on my site?" A research was conducted proving that selling all products on an ecommerce site without selecting a specific niche to focus on was a problem. In the sense that it costs more to market the products and it also took a long time. This is due to the high number of products being sold on the site. This makes it increasingly difficult to keep track with your dropshipping site and the fluctuation of the prices. In basic terms, it is hard to make a profit without a specific niche to focus on.

A good way to find a nice would be to make a list all of the things you have an interest in or have some knowledge in. In the long run, this will help you a lot further in the process when it comes to setting up and managing your store. The next step would be to work out what products you could sell in that category. For example, having an interest in Golf and selling Golf clubs, Golf Clothing, Accessories etc.

The next part comes down to pricing which is one core aspect of selecting a successful niche. I would advise you to choose products that have a price of around $300-$1000. If spending over $1000, customers usually want to first call in when placing large orders for products at that price and you want to minimize a number of calls that you will receive. You should note that the same amount of work is required when dropshipping a $20 product or a $500 product. Therefore, after putting a lot of effort the $20 seller tends to make less money than the $500 seller. It will be better for the dropshipper to market a product that sells for more than $300 as the returns are a lot higher for such products.

Now that you have identified the higher priced items, which niches or sub-niches do you think you could successfully dropship in? Start to think of suppliers for these products and move on to the next chapter.

If you are struggling to find high priced items then maybe the eBay or Aliexpress method is for you that we mentioned in the previous chapter.

When using platforms like Aliexpress to dropship, it is important to check customer ratings and reviews. This makes it a lot easier to determine which product is worth selling. It would be terrible to receive return after return. As we discussed earlier on, the quality of some goods from China can be hit and miss. Therefore, it will serve the dropshipper a great deal to do their due diligence and research the products they are looking at dropshipping. Reading the reviews should give you more information on the quality and whether the product is good for dropshipping or not. If you are unsure, you can always order items to your house to check as samples.

Finding and Contacting Suppliers

Now that you have decided to start a dropshipping business you need to find a supplier for your products. In the previous topic we delved in deep about niche markets and now it is paramount for us to also discuss the issue of finding a dropshipping supplier for your product. There is a high likelihood that more than one supplier sells your product online. You need to figure out which supplier is the best and the terms they will be offering for your product. Now you will need to figure out a way to contact the suppliers. A lot of Chinese suppliers cannot speak good English but the larger suppliers usually have an English speaking customer service team.

The best place to find and contact suppliers is on Aliexpress. Aliexpress is built in such a way that accommodates dropshippers. This means that you will not have a hard time as a dropshipper. First of all, you need to identify the product that you want to dropship. Let's say a dropshipper runs a website which dropships generators. In order to find suppliers on Aliexpress, he will first have to go to Aliexpress and search the generator sector. A list of generators shall appear and the dropshipper will choose the product that he/she wants. On every store, there is a tab that says Contact Now, this makes it simple for the dropshipper to contact the supplier.

You will know that it is possible to find a fake seller or a scammer on Aliexpress. Aliexpress has spent a lot of money trying to combat scammers. Therefore, it might not be the best idea to always choose the seller with the lowest ratings or pricing. I advise that you make a background check on all your suppliers. Aliexpress has started charging sellers $1500 to use the platform. This practice was done a lot to prevent fraudulent suppliers.

Be careful with suppliers selling branded products and always go with the suppliers that have a 95% plus feedback. The supplier must have at least 2000 sales. This will ensure that you are dealing with the most reliable suppliers.

Another tip I would suggest in finding a supplier will be to order a sample from the supplier in order to evaluate it. Product samples are very important when trying to find out the quality of your supplier's products. This can be a wise decision especially if you are a seller who has a large budget. Two to three samples will do the trick. After that, you will know if the supplier you have chosen is trustworthy and genuine. If your budget is low, however, you may want to skip this step.

Now let's focus on the part of communicating with the supplier. First, I would advise you to have a business email address. This helps as it will convince the supplier that you are a company that wants to do business with them. I would advise you not to use free email services such as yahoo.com, Hotmail.com, and gmail.com. These might be convenient when communicating generally, but they are not advisable when communicating in business terms.

The email is the first means of communication for a lot of dropshippers who want to contact suppliers. This is due to the fact that it's easier to get most of the information you want on the email than sitting on the phone. It is also cheaper to send an email than calling the supplier. Salehoo provides the dropshipper with a more professional email template so that the dropshipper might come out more professional. Another point to note is that you must not come out as a newbie. This will do much to discredit you to the supplier. The supplier needs to think that you have been in this industry for more than 5 years.

State your subject clearly. One thing you should not forget is stating your objective clearly and you need to make sure that it is catchy as possible. Imagine that these are suppliers who receive more than 2000 orders a day, so most likely they have no time to read through all the emails they get. The subject nails the cross and draws the attention of the supplier.

Remember that first impressions are everything, therefore the first impression that you will give the supplier will determine the way that they will treat you so please do your best to come across as a professional company to deal with. Your emails should not have spelling and grammatical errors. This will improve your chances of having a good relationship with the supplier since you are going to be a repeat seller.

Although in this section I have focused more on suppliers like Aliexpress, there are other suppliers such as worldwidebrands.com. Worldwide brands have been in business since 1999. The best part of this supplier network is that they are a dropshipping oriented network and they are scammer free as all of their suppliers are first verified for authenticity. This is a positive in the world of dropshipping were a lot of dropshippers have lost customer funds.

Another amazing platform where dropshippers can find suppliers is on Salehoo. Salehoo was created by ecommerce store owners who were fed up of having a hard time finding good suppliers and also were tired of scammers. This site comes at a relief for most dropshippers to contact suppliers.

Here are some of the questions you might decide to ask.

1. What are the payment methods you accept?
2. Are they any cost besides the cost of purchasing the product?
3. How long does it take for the product to be shipped and received by the customer?
4. Do you have a return policy? If you have a return policy, what is it?
5. Do you inform the dropshippers when prices change?
6. Can you supply us with customs items?

These questions are very important as they make it clear the requirements of the dropshipper. You must be precise and straight to the point when communicating with the supplier. Remember to explain things clearly depending on your needs as a dropshipper.

Creating a Dropshipping Website

Creating a dropshipping site can be very cheap to do when compared to more traditional business models. It is a concept that requires only a small investment since there are now a lot of sites that can do all of the work for you. Creating a dropshipping website is not much different from creating a regular ecommerce website. Shopify is one platform that has caused the explosion in terms of ecommerce websites. Dropshippers are not left behind as the industry standard platform for dropshippers thanks to its low cost and many free and paid theme options available. Shopify has recognized that 33% of ecommerce sites are using the dropshipping method and they've allowed dropshippers to easily create and tailor a dropshipping store on their platform.

Step 1.

First, you will have to register on shopify.com. You will need to have a valid email address in order to do this. Shopify will then send you an email asking you to verify your email address.

Step 2.

After verifying the email, an information page will appear and you will have to fill in the electronic form. The form will require your name, surname, date of birth, location (city, country, and residential address).

Step 3.

After completing this form, you will be taken to your online store admin page. This is where the whole process becomes a bit tricky for first-time dropshippers. You will have to do some trial and error if you are a slow learner. This is basically the part where you build your online store into a proper store.

The cost to use Shopify for dropshipping varies. It generally ranges from $29 to $299 per month. The plans have different features. The plan you will choose has to suit your requirements. Most first-time Shopify users use the basic Shopify plan which costs $29. However, you should take note that Shopify has another plan called Shopify lite. This plan is only $9 per month. Unfortunately, this plan is not suitable for dropshippers as it does not support online point of sale purchases. Therefore, it would be wise for any dropshipper to stay clear away from this plan.

Shopify has a 14 day free trial for your store. This means that you can create your store and have it launched online for a period of 14 days for free. However, you cannot conduct any online sales with this type of free plan meaning that your customers are not able to purchase products online from your store.

I would advise any first-time dropshipper to choose the $29 Shopify plan as it is more affordable and offers most of the features that the dropshipper might want to use in their store. It includes features such as 2 staff accounts, an unlimited number of products, unlimited file storage, free SSL certificate, website, and blog. This will be the main plan that we will be using as an example in the dropshipping store creation. You can also register your .com domain name through Shopify.

Adding Products

Since we have dealt with the most of the registration part which involves signing up and choosing the right Shopify plan for our store, we can now go ahead and add products to our store. This process is probably the most important part of dropshipping. You need to select your products carefully and make sure that enter the correct prices. The prices need to take into account profits, shipping costs and cost to advertise the product.

The first button on the store's administration page is 'Add Products'. This is the button you are going to use when adding products to the Shopify store.

Click the Add Product button and you will be taken to a fill-in section where you will have to fill in details such as title, price, and description.

Because you are a dropshipper you can focus on searching for the products you want to dropship and simply copy and paste most of the details. It is advised that you change the description so it is unique as Google ranks unique content higher.

If you are using Aliexpress as your supplier, go and search the products that you want to focus on in a specific niche. For instance, in this case, I will focus on portable generators. Go to Aliexpress and type portable generators in the search tab. A list of portable generators will appear. Make sure you sort the products by the highest number of products first and check the supplier's feedback score. This way, you know the supplier is used to supplying these products and already has many happy customers.

Add the pictures from the Aliexpress supplier. Then click on Add Product. Your product will be automatically added to your store and your customers will be able to purchase it online. Repeat this process to add as many products as you can possibly can.

Customizing Your Store

Now it comes to choosing a theme that best suits the needs of your store. You will need to install a theme. Shopify has themes that are free but if you want to stand out from other dropshippers, I suggest that you go with a paid theme.

After selecting a theme you will have to customize your store. This involves changing the color and look of the theme you chose. Shopify will automatically add different sections to your site and you can add or remove them as you choose. It will come as a relief as it will ensure that your theme is perfect for your intended use.

The Shopify App Store has a collection of plug-ins that will help you improve the functionality of your site. It has plug-ins that will help you out with complex things such as accounting, email marketing and market your products on popular social network websites such as Facebook. These amazing plug-ins are necessary for the success of your dropshipping website. There are more than 1200 Shopify plug-ins. The most popular plug-in is Oberlo which when installed in your store will help you as a dropshipper to add products to your store from Aliexpress.

Aweber for Shopify is another awesome plug-in. This plug-in allows you to integrate your Shopify store with your Aweber account. It is mainly used for email marketing, allowing you to send bulk emails to customers according to shopping trends.

Shopify Product Review allows your customer to give you a feedback on the product they have just purchased. This is very convenient as it allows you to engage with your customers in order to provide better services and increase sales.

The Shopify Facebook plug-in allows you to directly sell your products on your Facebook page. This is an integral marketing theme for dropshippers. You will now be harnessing the power of a social media giant. This will likely increase traffic and sales to your website. The amount of traffic that will be directed to your website can lead to conversions.

Another popular plug-in is Order Printer. Order Printer allows you to create online invoices, receipts, and labels. This plug-in has a lot of different templates to use when printing these invoices and receipts for your dropshipping website.

After adding and removing sections of your theme, you can go ahead and launch your store. Make sure you make it as attractive as possible. Before you launch your site go to ecommerce grader. This is a feature on Shopify that corrects errors on your ecommerce site. It also helps you with SEO. Also, you will need to check your store's preview before you launch. This is to ensure that the look of the store is what you want. Make sure that you check this on all screen sizes and don't forget to optimize the look for cell phone users. Do not neglect this part of the process as a lot of shopping is done via mobile users these days.

After you have launched your store you can go ahead and start marketing it in order to get customers. This is probably the hardest part of launching an ecommerce store. It will determine whether your dropshipping business will be a success or a failure. Most dropshippers use Google Analytics to track the performance of their store.

Store Checklist

Now let us focus on your store's checklist after you have finished creating your online store. There are certain essential features that need to be present on your store for potential customers to believe that you are a professional and trustworthy business.

Make Your Online Shop Sell

In this first point, you need to ensure that you designed your shop so that it can sell. You need to make your shop sell products. There are some online sellers who make such terrible designs to the extent that their stores can hardly make a sale. You need to ask around from a few of your friends and colleagues to find out if your store looks attractive. This includes the theme that you have chosen, the color and the general layout of your store.

Did You Choose The Right Products?

You will need to show the customers that your products are worth their money. This comes without saying but the quality of products should match the customer's expectations for the price shown. You will need to make sure that you selected the right niche and product to sell on your website. Not every product you dropship will be accepted by your customers so you need to do a quick research on the products that you intend to sell on your store. Your main goal as a dropshipper is to show your customer the right products and make sales.

Build Trust Amongst Your Website Visitors

The most important thing when building a checklist for your website is to build trust amongst your website visitors. There are a thousand ways to do this. People are careful about what they spend their hard earned money on, therefore the products you will need to put up on your site should elicit good reviews.

Below are probably some of the features that will increase your website's usability, accessibility, and profitability.

Deals

Nothing does it like deals, freebies, and free shipping deals. This is probably the most effective strategy that will drive sales on your dropshipping website. Always make sure that discounts and hot deals are on the front page of your website's page. They need to be featured as good deals for your customer to purchase them. Free shipping has been proven to have a certain positive effect on sales. This makes it one of the best features to constantly include on your dropshipping website.

To reduce the burden on your dropshipping business you should include a minimum amount shopping list to include free shipping. For example, you can state that if a customer purchases 2 laptops for $500 they will be offered free shipping. This will increase your sales whilst reducing your losses. This is a good tactic used by many dropshippers.

Logo Design

Your website logo represents your business; therefore, you should always aim to create a clear good looking logo for your business. This will improve your chances of increasing your profits and sales over a long time. When people start trusting your logo they will begin purchasing more goods on your site. The logo is basically the face of the business. This makes it an irreplaceable feature you should pay close detail to. On sites such as Fiverr, you will be able to find freelancers that can create for your site good logos for relatively low prices. A customs logo can cost as little as $5 on Fiverr.

Theme

Always make sure that the theme that you have chosen compliments the niche that you are selling in. Also, when customizing your theme, you will need to make sure that it leaves a good appearance on your site. The theme is basically the look of your dropshipping website, therefore you can't take chances when selecting and customizing your theme. Remember not to add too many features on your website as it will create a complicated website to use and do a lot of harm on your site. Your site basically needs to have a simple theme and features in order to be usable. An example of a good website will be the apple store. The store has the basic necessities which make it easy for a lot of customers to purchase their products. Ensure that plug-ins are properly installed and function well.

Clear Pictures

All product pictures on your site should be clear and portray the product as it is. Do not put pictures with a low resolution or quality. This will put customers off from buying your products.

The Search Bar

The search bar has become standard on many sites these days. There is no place more important for this feature than on an ecommerce website. Imagine how difficult it will be to use eBay or Amazon if they did not have a search bar. This feature saves a lot of time for the customer. You should ensure that this feature is available on your site and that it functions perfectly. This is very important especially if you have added many products on your website. Your customer won't have to waste time searching for a product on your site.

About Us Page

The about us page is an important feature in building trust between you and your customers. It helps give your customers a brief outlook on who you are and what you stand for. In simple terms, it should be the welcome carpet to your site. In most Shopify themes this page already exists. If it doesn't exist then you will need to add it yourself. Just go to the Customize button and click on Add Page. Some customers will judge the integrity of your store using this page.

Return Policy

The most trustworthy ecommerce site has got a standard return policy. Remember to create a return policy that suits your requirements. For instance, it will be favorable to offer the customer a return policy that allows the customer to return the product if it doesn't match the specifications. Return policies always build trust and confidence on the ecommerce site.

Delivery Info

The delivery info should always be represented on the site. If you are dropshipping from Chinese suppliers, the delivery time will be much longer. If you are shipping via Aliexpress, you will need to inform your customers that the delivery might take anywhere up to 40 days. You should never understate the delivery times as this will only lead to customer complains further down the line. If the delivery times are clearly laid out, you can always refer to this if a customer asks why they haven't received their order yet.

Trust Guard

Shoppers don't usually trust websites that they are not familiar with. In order for shoppers to trust websites, the website needs to be popular. This is not a problem when you sign up for a trust guard certificate. A trust guard is a third party verification system which verifies the authenticity of a site in order to prevent fraud related activities. This kind of certificate helps you as a dropshipper to gain the trust of your customers and lets them know that they are protected. Using this also helps your search engine ranking.

Contact Us

The contact us feature is very important when it comes to dropshipping or any online store. Remember that sometimes your customers will need to contact you before making an order. This is especially vital with more expensive products. Therefore, you will need to ensure that this feature is available on your site. You can create a page for this feature. The page may include your postal address, phone number, Skype name and business email address.

How to Fulfill Orders

This is the part where dropshipping becomes totally different from other forms of ecommerce. Dropshipping involves a complex system of purchasing the product from the supplier after your customer has made the purchase on your store. To begin explaining this process you need to know the levels of the supply chain.

The Manufacturer

This is where the product is created. The majority of manufacturers do not sell their products directly to the customer. They go through other players in the supply chain until the product reaches the customer. When you are a reseller, it is advisable to buy products directly from the manufacturer as they tend to be far cheaper. This increases your profit margin. Most manufacturers have got purchasing minimums. For instance, if you go to Alibaba marketplace you will discover that the manufacturers there require the purchaser to order a certain minimum. In this case, you will need to find a manufacturer who is willing to operate with no minimum order quantities.

The Wholesaler

The wholesaler is second in the supply chain. The wholesaler purchases products in bulk from the supplier in order to sell them at a slightly higher price. The wholesaler, like the manufacturer, can also have a minimum order, however, the minimum order for the wholesaler is lower than the manufacturer's minimum order. The wholesaler mainly sells to the smaller retailers. To get around minimum order quantities, you should go for products that have a high retail price (over $300). These higher value orders are more worthwhile for the wholesaler or manufacturer. They won't mind sending single units as they can still make good margins compared to selling cheaper items that they have to sell in multiples of 10, 50, 100 etc.

The Retailer

The retailer mainly sells directly to the consumer. The consumer is the final destination of the goods.

You would notice that the dropshipper was not included in the supply chain. This is because any of the three players in the supply chain can act as a dropshipper. This means that dropshipping is only a service offered by any of the three players. This means that, as a dropshipper, a company will ship products on your behalf directly to the customer.

Now that we have cleared the air and explained the players, lets us focus on the ordering process.

The Entire Ordering and Fulfillment System

A dropshipping site called hi-techone sells laptops. A customer places an order on the store and pays using his credit card. The dropshipper sees the order for one laptop and goes to the manufacturer's site to place a similar order at a much lower cost. In this scenario, it is important that the dropshipper must always have funds in order to quicken the process. The process will be much quicker than the dropshipper having to wait for 2 working days for the customer's funds to reflect in his account.

The dropshipper then places the order for the laptop on behalf of the customer. Now the supplier, who in this case is the manufacturer, will ship the product directly to the customer's address. The dropshipper has to put the address of the customer and not his own address. This will help expedite the whole process. This is how the dropshipper fulfills the customer's order.

Sometimes, the dropshipper may arrange for the manufacturer to include a customs package for all products included in the shipment but change the sender details to include that of the dropshipper. Therefore, the labeling on the packages will reference that the product is being sent from the hi-techone warehouse.

Fulfilling orders doesn't come without its own problems. For instance, a first-time dropshipper asked what he should do if a client orders different products with different suppliers from his dropshipping website. This is quite a difficult situation as the delivery times will most likely vary. For instance, one product might arrive from another supplier in 6 days and another in 10 days. It's important to tell your customer that his delivery will not arrive at the same time, as they are being sourced from different manufacturers. This will help clear a lot of questions that the customer might have further down the line.

Having a Good Relationship with Your Suppliers

When it comes to ensuring that your customer's orders are fulfilled properly, you need to make sure that you build and maintain a good relationship with your suppliers. This will make it easier for you to complete your orders. This is possible especially when you're making more than

1000 orders from the supplier a month. The supplier might even ship the product before you pay for it. This is due to the trust that you would have built over time.

When we talk about a good delivery service in the dropshipping sector, we are mainly focusing on dropshipping fulfillments. You should make sure that your customer receives the product at precisely the timeframe that you state. This means that you should pick suppliers that are trustworthy and have a good reputation. It will do you no good to pick a supplier who always delivers late and this can only create many customer service calls and emails that you will need to respond to. The thing that the customer is mainly concerned about is getting his goods in a short space of time.

Dealing with Customers

Dealing with customers is a pivotal part of dropshipping that you won't be able to bypass if you intend to be successful in the business. Customers usually have a lot of queries that need to be answered about products and poor communication could jeopardize sales.

Customer Services

In the dropshipping business, customer service involves managing your customer's queries, questions, and concerns. This is a labor-intensive task especially when your business is growing and more customers are shopping from your website. The truth is that it is almost impossible to offer perfect customer service to all of your customers. This is due to the fact that you usually do not hold the merchandise that you sell. When you start dropshipping, a huge part of the customer experience is out of your control. Part of the experience rests in the hands of the supplier who ships the product. However, at the end of the day, you are the one responsible for your customer's experience. To the customer, you are not able to blame the supplier for any delays on an order.

This brings us to the main issue of dealing with your customers. Dealing with your customers can be a very difficult task as you are the person who has to be providing the answers to the customer's questions. Due to the fact that you do not hold the inventory that you are selling on your online store, it becomes difficult to answer questions for some of the products you are selling because you have not seen the product to check for any problems that may arise.

Virtual Assistant (VA)

We get into the dropshipping business for many different reasons, but having no time to do other things is not one of them. This brings us to the issue of virtual assistants. The virtual assistant is probably the first employee an ecommerce entrepreneur hires. A virtual assistant basically frees some of your time by allowing you to focus on mainly managing your website. A virtual assistant will do a lot of tasks such as Facebook marketing and engaging, customer services and most daily tasks.

The function of the virtual assistant is to take care of the daily tasks that are necessary for running a dropshipping business. First, you will need to know when it is appropriate to hire a virtual assistant and how to hire a virtual assistant.

When you reach the stage where you need to hire a virtual assistant, your dropshipping business will have reached a stage where it is now too large to be managed by one person. As ecommerce stores start receiving a lot of orders, there is a need for the dropshipper to hire virtual assistants to help in the day to day running of the business.

Virtual assistants are usually not permanent employees, but they provide necessary skills in the growth of your dropshipping business. One very important sector is customer services and marketing. Virtual assistants are good if you are running on a limited budget. They will perform most of your tasks for a low price. The best part is that they operate remotely. This means that you can hire virtual assistants from countries such as the Philippines to perform tasks such as online marketing, customer order fulfillment and to answer any questions that the customer might have. Usually, a customer might have a question before purchasing a product. The Virtual assistant has the responsibility to answer the many questions that the potential client may have.

Hiring a Virtual Assistant

There are factors that you must take note of when hiring a virtual assistant. Nowadays hiring a virtual assistant is as easy as going online and clicking a button. The website I would advise you to go to when hiring a virtual assistant is Upwork. There are a lot of experienced virtual assistants to choose from. You should always make sure you are hiring the virtual assistant who suits your requirements. For instance, if you want a customer service virtual assistant to be able to respond to your customer's emails then you need to make sure that the virtual assistant has the skills and experience for this role. Luckily, everyone on Upwork shows their previous job history on their profile with feedback from past employers. You can conduct a Skype video call in order to interview the virtual assistant.

Interviewing a virtual assistant is important before you hire them. You can send messages to them, but you need to validate the level of experience they have on the task they will have to accomplish. Then you will have to train the virtual assistant to log in and use your system to accomplish your customer's needs.

You will need to train your virtual assistant in the ways of dropshipping. There are techniques in training a virtual assistant. First of all, you need to establish proper communication channels. I will suggest you use both Skype and WhatsApp. The Philippines usually has a lot of virtual assistants who can speak fluent English. They are also affordable for a dropshipper who has a limited budget. First of all, you need to give the virtual assistant access to a staff account. This will allow the virtual assistant to deliver customer services as well as add products to your store and market the store.

The Virtual assistant should also be given lessons on order fulfillment as this will be core to your dropshipping business. The virtual assistant will need to place the orders made by the customer to the supplier. They will also have to act as a customer service professional as placing the order won't be enough. This involves answering any question that a prospective customer might have. A lot of this will have to be done manually and you will need to train your virtual assistant in all of the relevant aspects.

Your virtual assistant will have to respond to customers requests kindly and with respect. This will ensure that the customers feel welcome on your store. Since we have already emphasized the importance of customer services before, you will also have to implement good customer services in other sectors of your dropshipping business such as your social media platforms. Customer service is the pivotal part of your dropshipping business, therefore, you would have to make a good impression in this regard. Communication with your customers is very important when running a business of any kind.

How to Automate Your Store

We have previously discussed some of the hardships that are involved with running a successful dropship store, however, you will be glad to know that you can make things easier by automating your store. Store automation is the best way to make dropshipping a less labor-intensive venture. There are several ways to do this. However, you should know that you cannot entirely automate your store, as some things can only be done by humans. Amazon has introduced robots to ease work in its fulfillment center but there are still humans working there, doing the tasks that robots cannot do.

When some entrepreneurs think about dropshipping, they automatically think that dropshipping can provide some kind of passive income for them. This is not entirely true when it comes to having a profitable store. Just like any online store you will need to put in some work in order to be successful with dropshipping. Hard work always pays off so don't expect dropshipping automation to do all the work for you. This is not possible. You will need to do some tasks on your own.

There is a lot you can automate in your dropshipping store. This includes payment processing, order fulfillment and managing your inventory. There are many online apps that will help you do most of these tasks. Usually, there is more than one app for a task. This means you will have to select the software that best meets your demands. There are some tasks that you cannot automate like customer service. Customer services will be almost impossible to automate. This is due to the fact that you will most likely need to engage with your customers. Therefore, this is a task that can only be done by humans and an app.

Oberlo

Oberlo is the best way to start dropshipping with Aliexpress. The Oberlo app makes it easy for online ecommerce users to dropship their products.

So far, dropshippers have sold more than 85 million products through the app. This makes it by far the most popular automation method on the market.

Now let's explain what really makes Oberlo so valuable as far as dropshipping is concerned. Oberlo app is totally free. This means that dropshippers don't have to spend money to use the app and it replaces time-consuming work usually carried out manually. Dropshipping is a difficult task, but when it comes to automation, Oberlo does the trick. This is by far the best way to automate your dropshipping business.

However, as we said earlier on, it is impossible at the current moment to fully automate your dropshipping business. The part that Oberlo mostly automates is placing products on your website. Oberlo helps you to add products to your catalog automatically. All you have to do is select the products that you want to add to your store. You can call this semi-automation of the store.

Dropshipping using Oberlo is an easy task even for first-timers. This is due to the fact that most labor-intensive part of dropshipping can be handled by the Oberlo app. Many dropshippers will tell you that finding products then, copying the material such as pictures and description is the hard part.

First, you will need to create an ecommerce store using Shopify. Then, install Oberlo into your Shopify store. Oberlo will automatically be integrated into your store's admin page. Open Oberlo and click on the button Find Products. You will be taken to a search bar which allows you to find products in your niche. Let's assume that for this case our niche is Bluetooth speakers. This means that we need to find Bluetooth speakers. You will then use your web browser to search for Bluetooth speakers. An entire catalog of Bluetooth speakers will appear based on your search keywords. Now you will need to select the items that you want to sell. A lot of items will appear and my advice is that you choose items that have high ratings. This will ensure that there are a few returns that will occur and you are buying from a reputable source. This does not guarantee that they will be no returns. There are always returns no matter how good the product is.

Now you need to import these Bluetooth speakers to your catalog. Go to the Import List and check that there are no duplicated products, then click on Import The Products To Your Store. Automatically, your products will be transferred to your store with descriptions and photos copied over from Aliexpress. This is one of the best methods to automate your dropshipping business.

The Oberlo will perform a lot of tasks automatically and this will save you a lot of time and money. For example, Oberlo will keep an inventory count for you. This will ensure that there are no products that are being sold whilst the supplier is out of stock. Therefore, you will not need to be contacting the supplier to ask about the availability of the product you are selling on your dropshipping store. This is one of the best features of Oberlo that has made the application so popular amongst a lot of dropshippers.

Another function that makes Oberlo amazing is the price alteration. On Oberlo, you can now weigh in your profit percentage. This means that you can automatically stipulate what profit you would like to make from the sale of each product. For example, let's say we decide to sell Bluetooth speakers on our store and we want a profit of 20%. There is a multiplier on Oberlo which can be altered to represent the price you want to appear. A product that sells for $100 on Aliexpress can automatically appear with a price tag of $120 on your website. The only thing you need to do is change the multiplier to 1.20. This will become the uniform pricing for your entire store.

There is also a fulfillment feature in the Oberlo app. This does not fully automate the process, however, but I think you will find that going in and processing the orders once or twice a day is significantly quicker than going on to Aliexpress, ordering the stock, entering the customer's address in etc. The shipping status and tracking numbers for orders are also synced with Oberlo, saving even more time.

Inventory Source

This dropshipping platform was founded as early as 2002 and it can be easily called the pioneer of dropshipping automation. Inventory Source is very easy to use and is an important part of dropshipping automation. The platform is not free to use but there are different plans that a dropshipper can choose from in order to dropship their products. This can be a bit of a drawback for dropshippers who are working on a budget.

The site has a product line of more than 1 million SKU's and sourced from more than 100 quality suppliers. The best thing is that all of these suppliers are screened. This makes it easy for dropshippers to choose suppliers without most of the hassle. The best thing about this platform is security as most of the vetting will have been already done for you. This platform automates a lot of its functions such as product uploading and importing. It also updates price and features that may be changed by the supplier. This means that the dropshipper does not need to continuously follow up and update the price changes.

Etail Solutions

If you are a dropshipper that works on different platforms, then Etail Solutions is the right platform for you. It integrates all of your platforms such as Shopify and marketplaces such as Aliexpress and Amazon into one interface. This makes your work a little bit easy and less exhausting.

The software automates day to day tasks and reduces the need for the dropshipper to hire a person to do the tasks. It manages purchases and automatically fulfills orders. This is a one of a kind software for dropshippers. You can also keep your product catalog up to date using this software. All of this is done automatically.

This solution does not offer a trial period and it is not free. This is the only downside for this automation solution.

Inventory Automation

A huge part of dropshipping automation has to involve inventory automation. This is an important part of dropshipping as it allows the dropshipper to easily manage his or her inventory. As a dropshipper, you will not want to have an inventory that is not up-to-date or having to spend a large amount of time adding products to your catalog. The use of apps such as Oberlo has made this part one of the easiest in dropshipping. This enables the dropshipper to focus on other important aspects such as social media marketing.

As I have previously stated before. It is impossible to completely automate a dropshipping business. This is due to the fact that some tasks are better off completed by humans. Even large corporations such as Amazon cannot automate their entire business operation. This means that as a dropshipper you will need to hire someone to conduct the tasks that cannot be automated.

The best person to hire is known as a virtual assistant. It is actually very cheap to hire a virtual assistant if you source these people on sites such as Fiverr and Upwork where you can get a virtual assistant who is qualified in dropshipping. This means that the tasks that cannot be automated will now be done by a virtual assistant. This includes social media marketing and engaging public relations and dropshipping fulfillment and returns. Hiring virtual assistants is usually done when the dropshipping business is growing and the owner no longer has time to complete most of the task himself. You can hire virtual assistants to cover all of the day-to-day running of your dropship store.

Marketing Your Store

Marketing is probably one of the most important parts of any business. It is important for a dropshipper to apply one of the best marketing tactics in order to target the right customers. This means that the only way a dropshipper can achieve success is to apply the most effective marketing tactics.

There are many different marketing platforms that are suitable for dropshippers and most of them are done online. This is due to the fact that dropshipping is mostly an online business and all sales are conducted online. The dropshipper has to use a mixed combination of marketing platforms. Here, we shall focus on the many marketing platforms and their advantages and disadvantages. Online marketing platforms include Facebook marketing, Instagram, Google ads, Twitter, and email marketing.

First, before you apply any of the marketing platforms to your dropshipping business you need to undergo a pre-marketing strategy. This involves making sure that your website is usable and it looks professional for potential customers. In simple words, you need to convince your customers to purchase from your store. If your store does not look good then most likely you will have a hard time making a sale if any. Even if you sell the best products in the market, you still need to give your customers a reason to go into your store. In the modern economy, there is now an abundance of items and you need to focus on what you want to sell and how you would sell it. This means that you have to have a reason why the buyer should buy from your store.

The basic goal for marketing your dropshipping business is to direct more targeted traffic towards your store. Although you will also need to create conversions and sell off as many products as possible, you still need to direct traffic towards your store. You cannot make sales without sufficient targeted traffic.

Motivate Customers to Purchase from Your Store

Usually, during holiday seasons, customers are looking for bargains and discounts, therefore there is no better way to market your business than offering promotions on your site during holidays. This is how you motivate customers to buy from your site. You need to create a sense of urgency that will make a customer want to make a purchase on a limited time offer. They don't want to wait till the promotion period is over, therefore they are most likely to take action on the offered promotion or discount.

Facebook Advertising

Now let's focus on one of the best marketing platforms in the industry. Facebook marketing is perhaps the most important form of marketing you will need to learn as a dropshipper. Facebook has more than 1.2 billion active users. This means that as a dropshipper, you will be able to put your product in front of 1.2 billion potential buyers. This factor alone makes Facebook one of the most sort after dropshipping marketing methods on the internet.

Facebook has an awesome online Facebook ads service that allows you to direct paid traffic to your website. As a first-time dropshipper, I would advise that you use Facebook ads instead of trying to advertise your store on your own. This saves a lot of time and it is highly effective.

Facebook advertising has basic components and functions that you would need to pay close detail towards. These include setting the objective of the Facebook campaign, targeting a certain group of people. You should remember that any of the criteria that you will choose such as age, gender and location will determine whether your dropshipping business will be a success or failure.

How to Use Facebook Ads

Now let's focus on how to use Facebook Ads. We will be mainly focusing on paid ads. Promoting your store on Facebook is probably the best step you can take towards dropshipping success as you can reach the people most likely to buy from your store. I should mention that this might come as a difficult task but it is very necessary when it comes to promoting your dropshipping business. The first thing you have to focus on is the kind of population segment you want to promote your site to. I usually tell most dropshippers to narrow their demographic down to the bare minimum. This will make it a bit easy to drop ship their products and get more sales.

The most important part to consider when deciding to use Facebook ads is your budget. This will basically affect the number of people your ad is going to reach and their location. Usually, ads in places such as Mexico are actually cheaper than ads in places such as the United States on average. Again focusing on a much larger audience also makes the ad costs more expensive. As far as Facebook ads marketing is concerned there will be a lot of trial and error. This means you will need to be readjusting your budget as you learn and discover new things.

Targeting the right audience is the first thing you will have to consider in creating your Facebook ad. Not to push stereotypes here but a 60-year-old factory worker in Russia is the least to target when selling sanitary pads. For such a product you will most likely want to focus on young women.

Let's say you are dropshipping in a niche such as drones suitable for children. Then you would need to focus on the geography that is most likely willing to purchase those drones. This means you will select a population in the United States such as California. Then you need to narrow it down to the age that is most likely going to purchase the drones. Select ages from 22 to 65 assuming that parents might want to buy drones for their children. As a dropshipper, you need to be very considerate of the target that you select to promote the products to. You need to select the appropriate dropshipping audience to target specifically for your required niche. This will involve choosing the right age range, interest, hobbies, occupation etc.

You can then choose to promote your website as a Facebook page or to directly promote your website. You need to select a proper dropshipping budget. As far as the budget is concerned you should always remember to test what works for your site. This will involve changing demographics and daily budgets to ensure that you get the maximum out of your dropshipping business.

Instagram Marketing

The platform that has risen in popularity over the past few years is Instagram marketing. There are more than 600 million Instagram users around the world so this makes the platform an integral part of social media marketing. Instagram marketing can be tackled through many different ways such as paid promotion, and Instagram influencers marketing. Instagram Influencer marketing will be the main strategy you will need to focus on as a dropshipper.

Instagram influencers are a very effective way of marketing your dropshipping business. Considering that most people who will buy your product are people who are not personally affiliated with you, therefore this method will serve as the best method for marketing your store.

Instagram influencers are Instagram users who have a large following that might be interested in your product. Usually, most of these users have followers in the thousands or millions. Now as a dropshipper you will need to identify the best Instagram followers that suit your niche products. For example, it will be better to use Instagram followers such as models for fashion products that you are selling. Models will be better at representing your brand than a miner would.

Due to the fact that Instagram influencers have a large following, you are most likely going to make sales from them than marketing your Instagram page by yourself. The first step in Instagram influencer marketing is to find the right Instagram influencer and reach out to them. Reaching out to the influencer is a process whereby you communicate with the influencer and tell them that you want to market your products or store on their Instagram account.

A quick way to find Instagram influencers is to use platforms such as Ninja Outreach and Snapfluence. You will be able to target influencers that are directly in your niche. Now in order to communicate with these influencers, you will need to send them a direct message if you don't have their email address. It's advisable to use a professional email format than a personal email format. The influencer is more likely to take someone with a business email seriously than someone with a personal email like Gmail or Hotmail. Make sure you come out as professional as possible.

The costs of using Instagram influencers can be quite high than using Facebook marketing. Instagram influencers can charge from 100$ to $50000 depending on the size of the audience. This implies that the more Instagram followers an influencer has, the more money they are going to charge. An Instagram influencer like Kim Kardashian can charge as much as 1 million dollars for a single post. This is because such celebrities have a large following and are very popular on the entertainment scene. As an influencer, they know how valuable they can be to another business by promoting their products or services.

However, you are most likely going to look for cheaper Instagram influencers and not the Kardashians. Depending on your budget I would probably advise you to use Instagram influencers that have a modest following such as ten thousand or more. These are most likely going to produce good results for your social media marketing campaign. Influencers that charge around $500 per post are quite good for a first-time dropshipper. The best advice is to make sure that you do not overspend on one influencer. It is better to use several influencers for your dropshipping business. This will ensure that you have a broad platform and therefore lots of sales.

Building a Following on Your Own

Instagram marketing is effective when you start building a following on your own store. The first thing you will need to do is to sign up for Instagram and create an account where you will be posting pictures and content of your store. Now you will need to build a large following for the Instagram marketing to be effective enough to get sales. You can do this on your own without paid marketing tactics but it will be a slow process.

This means that you will have to post interesting contentment ranging from videos to pictures. Build your audience slowly beginning with your local friends and associates. You can then focus on telling your friends to advertise your Instagram account on your behalf. Now when it comes to posting interesting content, you need to use the most effective method on social media. This is the hashtag. Hashtags are actually very effective especially on social media these days. As a dropshipper, you do not need to only use hashtags that correspond to the content you are posting. This means that any form of a hashtag can be used to get followers on your store's Instagram page. I would suggest using trending hashtags. Trending hashtags are effective when it comes to getting a following on Instagram. Instead of just using any kind of hashtags people tend to want to click on trending hashtags than those that are not trending this makes them lucrative to you as a dropshipper.

Finding trending hashtags on Instagram is quite easy. You need to use a free tool such as Webstagram and check trending hashtag for a certain niche. You can also check trending hashtags for your keywords on other social media platforms. Instead of using Webstagram you can go on Twitter and select a specific region where you want to market your product copy the hashtags. This works well as a lot of people will end up visiting your post through the hashtag.

Another brilliant way to get Instagram followers is by siphoning followers from your competitors. It is well known that if a person follows your competitor they are interested in the product that you are selling. Therefore it will be advisable to simply get them to follow your account as well. The simple way to get these users to follow your store as well is to go to your competitor's account and find the followers then you need to engage with them by following them, commenting on their pictures, and liking their content. This is an effective way of building a following on Instagram and therefore getting more sales on your Instagram page.

Twitter Marketing

You can also use Twitter as a marketing tool. Twitter has more than 400 million active users as of 2017. The unfortunate part is that Twitter has been decreasing in popularity over the past few years. However, it is still a force to be reckoned with. The best part about Twitter is that it contains 54% of people who earn more than $50000 USD. This means that as far as marketing your products is concerned, you will have a much easier time finding buyers who can afford to visit your store.

The platform is best used if you want to create brand awareness for your store. The best part about Twitter is that you can also use Twitter influencers. Influencers will help you get more followers on your Twitter account. The cost to use an influencer on Twitter is cheaper than the cost of influencers on Instagram. This is a bonus if you intend to use Twitter influencers to market your store.

The main thing that sellers or companies always strive for in social media marketing is to get their product in front of the eyes of many people. This they hope will result in more sales and higher profits. Twitter tends to do the trick. The best feature on Twitter is the trending bar. When you use the trending bar for a certain location you intend to market your store it becomes easy on Twitter as you can simply use the hashtag to draw a lot of customers to your store. A lot of views might lead to the sales that you want. Twitter also has paid ads like Facebook but these paid ads are very expensive so they are mostly used by corporations.

Email Marketing

Email marketing is probably the oldest form of social media marketing. It has existed since the advent of email and nowadays, it has become a very popular marketing strategy especially for ecommerce stores. Even large companies such as Netflix, eBay, and Amazon use email marketing in order to increase their sales. Email marketing is simply the use of emails in order to make sales. In the case of a dropshipping store, this will be contacting existing customers and making them aware of new products, promotions etc. You will gather their email addresses when they placed orders through your site.

There are certain problems with email marketing that you will need to avoid. The first one is avoid spamming your customers. Email spamming usually annoys customers and forces them to unsubscribe from your email list. This is whereby you begin sending them a lot of emails that they are not interested in. This might make your entire email marketing campaign a failure.

Using Aweber

The best and most popular email marketing campaign tool is Aweber. Aweber is one of the easiest systems to use for email marketing. Aweber is used to get more subscribers, therefore; you get more prospective customers through this system. The best part is that Aweber is integrated with Shopify. This makes it a valuable part of marketing your dropshipping business. Aweber automatically generates signup forms that allow you to take the emails of prospective buyers.

To begin using Aweber you will need to sign up to a new Aweber account. Aweber is not free by the way, therefore, you will need to select a plan that best suits your requirements based on the scale of your business. For a new business, I will suggest you start with the $19.99 a month plan which allows you to use the Aweber services until you have 500 subscribers. The monthly plan price increases depending on how many subscribers you have. The next level up is $29 a month with up to 2500 subscribers. The most expensive Aweber plan is the pro marketer plan. This plan is specifically targeted at large businesses and businesses which are in the marketing sector. It costs $149 per month to use this plan but you can have up to 25000 subscribers. This plan basically is meant for high volume senders, especially those who have a lot of bulk emails to send to their clients. It also has analytic report system where you can compare and analyze the outcomes of your email marketing campaigns. This is another plus for the dropshipper.

Google Adsense

No one can start selling anything online without knowing about Google ads. Google ads have become synonymous with online ecommerce stores. This is a fantastic service provided by Google. This is due to the fact that the Google website is the most visited website in the world receiving more than 5 billion daily page views from users all over the world. This makes it by far one of the most lucrative forms of online advertising. As a dropshipper, I would advise you to make Google ads one of the first paid advertising methods you should use.

Adsense is the easiest tool to use in advertising and it is probably one of the most efficient tools. The first thing you should know is that Google ads are not free and you would need to organize a steady budget. The first thing you have to consider is the keywords. Google keywords are not the same price. Some keywords, especially in the field of finance, are more expensive than others. This means that you should also select niche keywords that are less pricey. Google has a research tool called Google AdWords which can be used for this. Google AdWords can be used to show the competitiveness of a certain niche and the amount of traffic that it receives including CTR which is the click-through rate. Click through rates are the number of people that on an ad over the number of impressions an ad receives.

Also, do not forget to select the type of ads you want for your ad campaign. There are different types of ad campaigns. There is the pay per click ad campaign and pay per 1000 impressions. There is another less popular one, which is pay per acquisition. All of these campaigns are suitable for different types of businesses. For dropshipping, we will be focusing on the PPC and the CPM which means you pay for every 1000 impressions. The M stands for one thousand in Roman numerals.

Costs vary between the different types of marketing campaigns. The costs per click can range from $1 per click to as much as $100 per click. It all depends on the niche that you are advertising in. Niches in the finance sector basically have a high cost per click and general niches have a lower cost per click than most niches. Therefore, as a dropshipper, it is important to choose the right keywords also taking into account the different price ranges associated with these keywords.

For dropshipping, I would advise you to use pay per click. This is due to the fact that it is most effective when you want to get sales on your dropshipping sales. This is by far the single best online marketing method because it allows you to choose the demographics and the budget that you intend to use for your campaign.

Other Ways to Boost Sales

Boosting your sales is a vital part of dropshipping because without sales you cannot achieve success. Apart from the methods that we have already explored there are still other methods of boosting your sales. You will need to use as many methods as suits you to boost your sales.

Use Scarcity

Have you ever visited a website and started searching for a hotel room and then you found a lot of hotels labeled filling up? This happens all the time. Sometimes you see listings marked as almost full. This is a marketing strategy that creates the need for immediate action from the buyer.

Using the scarcity method in order to convince the customer to buy your product is a very smart decision that you can take. This is due to the fact that it creates a sense of urgency in the customer's mind. If you are going to apply this technique make sure that it is legit because there is nothing as annoying as buying something limited and arriving two days later only to find the product available at the same price.

Sometimes you might decide to use a countdown timer. However, you have to be ethical when applying a countdown timer. There are many types of countdown timers that are applicable to dropshippers. You might simply put the number of products that remain or use more complex countdown timers such as time left for the promotion to end. You can put a price discount in this place, such as a 20% discount and then an ethical timer.

Discount Coupon Codes

Discount coupons are also an important part of dropshipping. This is probably one of the most common forms of boosting your online sales. Coupon codes are an effective way to attract new customers. As a dropshipper, you will have to give out coupon codes in order to get more sales. For example, you might offer discount coupon codes to first-time customers who buy certain products from your store.

You need to perfect the technique of offering discount coupons without hurting your own profits or incurring losses on your side. This will also ensure that your prices are lower than the competitors on in the market. Ecommerce shop owners usually place discount coupons to items that are not making a sale. However, as a dropshipper, you don't hold any inventory, therefore, the issue of items that are not selling is out of the picture.

How to Set Discount Price on the Store

Usually, online sellers want customers to know the original price before they put the product for a discount. This is a widely used strategy by online sellers. This can be seen even on popular ecommerce sites such as Amazon and Aliexpress. Showing the customer the original price, then slashing it will have the psychological effect desired on the customer. This means that you will be able to make more sales through convincing your customer that they are getting a good deal. That's what a customer usually wants, quality and a good price.

Now let's get to the whole process of setting up this discount price. On Shopify, there is the compare price section. You should make sure that the value of the compare price is higher. This will appear on your store as the original price which will be crossed over. Then after that, you can go ahead and write the price. Save the prices. The price should be lower than the compare at price. Now your price will appear as the discount price and the compare price as the original price before the discount.

Plug-Ins That Will Help You Boost Sales

Plug-ins are an integral part of making sales on your dropshipping site. Here are some of the awesome Shopify plug-ins that will make you generate a lot of sales on your store.

Plug-in SEO will simply help you with your store's search engine optimization. This plug-in specifically deals with making your store appear on search engines. Therefore, you have to make it part of your site in order to boost sales.

Facebook Share lets you sell products directly on your Facebook page. This plug-in is totally free when using Shopify. Therefore, you can now reach more Facebook users and sell your product to more customers around the world.

There is also the **Free Shipping Bar.** This is perhaps the most important plug-in for boosting sales on your dropshipping business. As the name of the app sounds the app allows you to show products that have free shipping. Most customers would love to purchase a product that has free shipping, especially free international shipping. It also allows you to "Free Shipping" messages on the cart when the customer is purchasing a lot of items.

To make your business look more professional, **Orderprint** is a good app to install. It allows you to print invoices, labels, and receipts to customers.

Exit Strategy

Now let's focus on the exit strategy. Every business owner needs an exit strategy that is in line with their business. Some dropshippers might wonder why one needs an exit strategy for a business that is successful and accumulating profits. There are a lot of reasons why a business owner might want an exit strategy at hand. The first reason being that as an entrepreneur you love the fun of a start-up so by the time you reach 10 employees, all that excitement would have disappeared. Another reason is that a larger company might offer a large sum of money that is very difficult to resist.

In about five years you will be anxious to start a new entity, therefore, you will no longer have time to focus on your dropshipping business. A lot of dropshippers seek an exit strategy when their business operation has become very large.

Merger and Acquisition

This is probably by far the most common exit strategy used by businesses. As the term suggests, the main thing you need to be concerned about is merging with another business and then removing yourself from the daily running of the business. Or being bought out by a much larger company. In this case, your business will no longer be a legal entity. This means the larger company takes over the running of the business.

Mergers and acquisitions are popular in the hi-tech start-up market as large technology companies battle to acquire strategic small start-ups. This has been seen in large companies such as Google, Facebook, and Microsoft. Over the past few years, these companies have been purchasing smaller start-ups at a high rate. This method is not favorable to most dropshipping businesses but it can also be used as an exit strategy.

Sell Your Business to an Individual

Most people usually confuse this exit strategy with an acquisition. This is not the same because this form of strategy is not combining two firms into one. This is the exit strategy that we will be mostly paying attention to as dropshippers. It is simply selling off your business to another entity or person. Some people would most likely want to buy a business than to start a new one from scratch. In this case, you will most likely use popular websites such as Flippa and Shopify Exchange to sell your website.

Make the Dropshipping Business Your Cash Cow

Another step you can take is to make the dropshipping business your cash cow. This means you can hire someone to run your dropshipping business for you whilst you focus on doing other important stuff. This is another highly favored exit strategy as most dropshippers develop an attachment to their business and it becomes very hard for them to let go of their business operation. In this case, you will be making money out of the business without having to run the business yourself.

Closing Shop and Liquidating Your Business

This is probably the least popular exit strategy. Some entrepreneurs can decide to close their business as they decide they have enough money to retire or to do what they always wanted to do with their life. This exit strategy is unlikely with a lot of dropshippers as there is no money tied up within the business.

The main idea behind exiting a business is not to get out of a terrible situation but to take advantage of a good situation. This means that as a dropshipper you should not exit when your business is bad, but exit when your business is most lucrative. The next section will focus on how you can sell off your business to a buyer.

How Much Is Your Dropshipping Business Worth?

The first and foremost task you need to take in selling your dropshipping business is to figure out how much your dropshipping business is actually worth. This task will help you sell your business at precisely the right price. The most important question to answer is why sell your profitable business?

There are a lot of reasons why dropshippers sell their business. It could be to reinvest the money in other business ventures. Some sell in order to transfer their online assets into physical assets such as property. Whatever the reason for selling your dropshipping business you need to first figure out the value of your dropshipping business.

A profitable dropshipping business can sell for as much as 20 times its monthly profit. There are a lot of factors that determine why a dropshipping business will sell for this much. Some of the factors that will determine this are the store's appearance on Google webpage, its Alexa rankings, and reliable suppliers.

The biggest factor to that will determine the value of your business will be the net monthly income. This is the income after you have subtracted the costs for running the business. The costs include product costs, staff, marketing, and costs to run the website.

Selling Your Dropshipping Business on Flippa

Flippa.com is the number one marketplace for selling websites and applications. The platform has made hundreds of millions of sales. It is also very popular so I can think of no other place for you to sell your business. There are many features on Flippa that make it very easy to use.

You will need to sign up for your website and fill in the required fields. Then you can proceed to post your website to the online platform. You can post it as a classified ad or as an auction. I would personally advise you to post it as an auction. In this case, you will have the option to include the buy now price. This makes it simple for the customer to avoid the auction and simply purchase the website if they want to. The reserve price is usually the minimum price that the seller is willing to sell the site for and the Buy Now price is the maximum price.

Conclusion

Dropshipping has risen in popularity over the past decade. This has mainly been fuelled by the increasing popularity of ecommerce stores. In the modern era, it has become common for people to purchase almost anything online. Nowadays people purchase food, electronics, and medical supplies online. Although this has not destroyed conventional shopping it has certainly increased the number of dropshipping businesses.

It is estimated that 33% of all ecommerce business are now using a dropship supply chain strategy. Even large corporate companies such as Walmart are involved in dropshipping operations in order to increase the amount of inventory they can sell to their customers.

As a dropshipper, you need to direct a lot of your funds on marketing your store and products. This is because you don't hold any of the products that you sell. Therefore, effective social media campaigns have to be employed. Hence, you need to market your store on popular sites such as Facebook, Instagram, and Google. Effective marketing campaigns on these websites are not free. It is advisable to commit a large amount of your budget on these websites.

In order to make dropshipping less labor intensive and time consuming it will be an excellent decision to use plug-ins that automate your store. These will free you from the time-consuming tasks that can be done by plug-ins such as Oberlo. You can even hire a Virtual Assistant on Upwork to complete some tasks that cannot be automated.

With all these benefits and potential earning I see little reason for an entrepreneur not to start a dropshipping business. The best part is that start-up capital is less, as you don't need to stock the products you are selling. This is what attracts a lot of entrepreneurs to become dropshippers.

Finally, if you enjoyed this book, please take the time to share your thoughts and post a review on Amazon. It would be greatly appreciated!

www.ingramcontent.com/pod-product-compliance
Lightning Source LLC
Chambersburg PA
CBHW070250230526
45470CB00002B/554